D1178396

Heitzmann, William Ray
14

The Newspaper in the Classroom

Second Edition

by Wm. Ray Heitzmann

nea PROFESSIONAL LIBRARY
National Education Association
Washington, D.C.

ACKNOWLEDGMENTS

The author would like to thank the following for their contributions to the second edition: Cynthia Armitage, *The County Press;* Suzanne Troxel, principal, SS. Peter and Paul School, Easton, Maryland; Margaret T. Buchholz, publisher/editor, *The Beachcomber* (New Jersey); Linda Skover, Manager, Educational Services, American Newspaper Publishers Association; Bob Vetrone, *Philadelphia Daily News;* Tony Leodora, *Times-Herald* (Pennsylvania); Mike Houldin, managing editor, *The Catholic Standard and Times*; Rosa Stefanesen, teacher, Grays Lake School District, Illinois; Villanova University; and his family.

Printing History:
First Edition: July 1979
Second Edition: January 1986

Note

Library of Congress Cataloging-in-Publication Data

Heitzmann, William Ray.
    The newspaper in the classroom.

    (What research says to the teacher)
    Bibliography: p.
    1. Newspapers in education.   I. Title.   II. Series
LB1044.9.N4H44   1986   371.3'2   85-25816
ISBN 0-8106-1066-3

CONTENTS

The Author

Wm. Ray Heitzmann, a member of the faculty of Villanova University, has had a long-time interest in developing basic process skills. He believes effective use of the newspaper in the classroom to be one of the most efficient techniques for assisting students in building basic skills. He admits to learning to read through the *Dispatch* and the *Jersey Journal*, two northern New Jersey newspapers.

Dr. Heitzmann is the author of several books, articles, and scholarly papers. These include *Minicourses*, *Educational Games and Simulations*, and *The Classroom Teacher and the Student Teacher*, published by NEA. His *Fifty Political Cartoons for Teaching U.S. History* (J. Weston Walch Publishers) and *Political Cartoons* (Scholastic Publishers) have been used by teachers working with newspapers in the classroom.

AUTHOR'S PREFACE
TO THE SECOND EDITION

The explosion of interest in developing basic process skills among children and adults has catapulted the newspaper into a valuable teaching aid. As a result, the newspaper can make an important contribution to learning.

Historically, educators have used the newspaper in two ways: teaching about it (product orientation), and using it to teach information to build skills (process orientation).

A product-oriented approach involves teaching students about the newspaper's various components—for example, what differentiates a newsstory from an editorial, how to read the classified advertisements, what is a by-line, how to interpret an editorial. Such instruction usually occurs throughout the curriculum, increasing in sophistication as students move through the grades. A successful strategy has been to devote a one-week unit in seventh grade and a two-week unit in tenth grade to studying about the newspaper. These units normally are a part of the Language Arts/English curriculum, but elements may be included in the Social Studies program.

The present emphasis in classroom use of the newspaper is on developing student skills. Teachers are successfully helping students improve in a wide variety of subject areas: arithmetic students are developing computational skills, science students are examining the newspaper for new advances, reading students are expanding their comprehension skills, and budding linguists are adding to their cultural knowledge by clipping current events about the countries whose languages they are studying.

The Newspaper in Education (NIE) movement has expanded among newspapers coast to coast. Desiring to work with and assist teachers as well as to sell their newspapers, many publishers have started and expanded NIE programs. NIE representatives have made a major contribution to the use of the newspaper in the classroom by providing teachers with classroom materials, conducting workshops on suggested instructional procedures, and offering field trips to newspaper offices. Not confined to the major dailies, the movement encompasses many small publications such as the *Auburn Evening Star* (Indiana), the *Pottsville Republican* (Pennsylvania), *The Temple Daily Telegram* (Texas), and *The Waterbury Republican* (Connecticut), which provide excellent services to schools.

The growth of this movement can be seen in the support of its annual observance. In 1985, 34 governors and 135 mayors proclaimed March 4–8 "NIE Week." During that period schools used more than one and one-half million newspapers.

A blizzard of reports and studies has criticized the skills of students. Among the tools available to classroom teachers, the newspaper stands ready to meet the challenge of maximizing students' abilities.

NEW RESOURCES FOR THE SECOND EDITION

Activity Cards (1983). *Lawrence Eagle-Tribune,* Box 100, Lawrence, MA 01842. Nine sets of activity cards (40 cards each set) organized by subject areas and emphasizing survival skills.

Adding Life to Math and Science (1983). *Deseret News,* Box 1257, Salt Lake City, Utah 84110. Math and science activities organized by topics to supplement regular lessons.

Basics in Balancing Your Budget (1983). *State Times and Morning Advocate,* P.O. Box 588, Baton Rouge, LA 70821. Introduces students to basic budgeting principles and the use of the newspaper as a valuable financial planning tool.

Elections: '84 : America Votes (1984). *USA Today,* P.O. Box 500, Washington, DC 20044. An activity booklet to study the presidency and political parties.

Filaroff, Joan, ed. *Newspaper Activities: Upper Level* (1983). *Austin American-Statesman,* Box 670, Austin, TX 78767. A series of instructional materials in several subject areas.

Heitzmann, Wm. Ray. *Political Cartoons* (1980). Scholastic Publishers, 902 Sylvan Avenue, Englewood Cliffs, NJ 07632. A valuable tool for teaching students the technique of interpreting political cartoons; contains color transparencies, spirit masters, and a teacher's guide.

Holidays in the News (1983). Wisconsin NIE Committee, c/o *Milwaukee Journal-Sentinel,* Box 661, Milwaukee, WI 53201. A "holiday curriculum" lesson for middle school students using the newspaper.

Know Your Newspaper (1983). *News-Tribune and Herald,* 424 West First Street, Duluth, MN 55801. An activity-style booklet that introduces students to the newspaper.

The Newspaper Approach to the Basic Essential Skills Test (BEST) (1980). *Kansas City Times/Star,* 1729 Grand, Kansas City, MO 64108. Publication focusing on newspaper-related activities organized around specific objectives.

NIE Starter Kit (1983). *The Spectator,* 44 Frid Street, Hamilton, Ontario L8N 363. Canadian-published materials containing a wide range of activities using the newspaper in the classroom.

Olsen, Marilyn. *News School: Using the Newspaper to Teach Social Studies* (1985). Dale Seymour Publications, Box 10888, Palo Alto, CA 94303. One hundred reproducible activities to enhance student skills; may be used with any daily newspaper.

Science Education Series (1983). *Newsday,* Long Island, NY 11747. Relates science to the daily newspaper—a ready source of science information and the scientific method.

Short, J. Rodney, and Dickerson, Bev. *The Newspaper: An Alternative Textbook* (1980). Pitman Learning, Inc., 19 Davis Drive, Belmont, CA 94002. Identifies skills the newspaper can develop and examines the newspaper as a product.

Using the Newspaper to Reinforce Reading and Writing Skills (1983). Florida NIE Coordinators, P.O. Drawer 2949, Ft. Walton Beach, FL 32549. A guide for educators working with third and fifth graders in basic skills areas.

INTRODUCTION

The flexibility of the newspaper has long made it an attractive instructional tool for classroom teachers. Educators have used the newspaper as a motivational device to develop basic skills and to promote learning in various subject areas. Additionally, some instructors (primarily those in language arts, English, and social studies) have integrated the study of the newspaper into their courses.

As a result of this interest and as a reaction to the expansion of television during the 1950s, many newspapers hired educational specialists to work with teachers in promoting the use of this medium in the classroom. Some of these programs have been in existence several years. The program of the *New York Times* dates back to the early 1930s.

The original concern of newspaper educators regarding the negative impact that television would have upon the reading skills and habits of young people has been realized. Almost daily, articles appear by researchers providing testimony to the increasing time children spend watching TV. For this and other reasons, educators in increasing numbers are working to build the reading habit. For example, many schools have adopted the SSR program—Sustained Silent Reading (also known as USSR—Uninterpreted Sustained Silent Reading). At a designated time each day, the entire school—principal, maintenance staff, cafeteria workers, teachers, and students—reads for a certain number of minutes.

Two organizations have served nationally as a focus for using the newspaper in the classroom: the American Newspaper Publishers Association Foundation (ANPA) and Visual Education Consultants (VEC). The former acts as a coordinating agency for Newspaper in Education (NIE) programs. "It develops and distributes materials, sponsors conferences for developing NIE programs, and advises individual schools and programs." (1) Several hundred newspapers serve thousands of schools. To realize its objectives, the program aims to:

> Help students become informed and involved citizens who can determine and guide their own destinies in a democratic society.
> Help students develop skills of critical reading by teaching competence in newspaper reading.
> Provide educators an economical, effective, and exciting teaching vehicle for lessons in writing [about] history, mathematics, current events, consumer affairs, ecology, and scores of other subjects.

Convey an understanding of the free press as an essential institution in a free society.

Foster students' personal growth through the use of the newspaper to provide information, entertainment, and skills necessary for modern life. (1) *

Originally established in 1952 as a small operation in the Midwest, VEC has expanded to 325 newspapers and more than 2¼ million students in North America. Richard De Prima, president of VEC, cites the following general goals of the program: (1) teaching about the newspaper; (2) using the newspaper in the standard curriculum; and (3) building a continuing newspaper habit. The organization believes that as a special instructional tool the newspaper has the following value to teachers:

FIRST—The daily newspaper is the most effective means yet found of spanning what has been called the "textbook lag." In each curriculum area, it bridges the gap between textbooks and the new developments that outrace their contents. Textbooks simply cannot be written, published and selected fast enough to keep pace with today's "knowledge explosion." The daily newspaper reinforces the academic textbook by linking yesterday and today.

SECOND—The newspaper is by far the most important chronicle of society ever invented. It is a living, daily record of a living, changing world. From births and obituaries, to want ads, to news pages, to comics—it is a mirror of the society in which students will spend the rest of their lives. (26)

This publication will provide practical suggestions based upon research findings and the experience of successful newspaper activities.

---

*Numbers in parentheses appearing in the text refer to the Selected References beginning on page 29.

CLASSROOM DISCUSSION

Successful teachers have long incorporated classroom discussion into their teaching. This technique, with its potential to build oral communication and critical thinking skills, works particularly well with newspapers, which constitute a reservoir of springboards to discussion.

In recent years, classroom interaction has become the subject of much interest and study. (29) Research on this teaching method has shown it to be an excellent device in stimulating a desire to learn. Studies have related classroom interaction to leadership style and have demonstrated that successful classroom climates, in which students participate in discussions, are related to student achievement. Teachers who respect students' feelings and ideas and encourage their responses have classrooms that promote learning. (29) Other studies have positively correlated critical thinking (5) and cognitive growth with teachers' questions, particularly with higher-level interrogatories. (51)

A major study that was carefully controlled involving twelve classes examined the question of whether newspapers increase the verbal participation of students. The researchers concluded that "significant increases in the proportion of student talk occurred in classes using the newspaper when compared with classes using regular textual materials." (29)

The educational community has moved away from the passive approach to classroom instruction to an emphasis on student activity. Using the newspaper as an instructional tool encourages discussion and student involvement. In this report, the sections on elementary education and subject areas contain several specific suggestions for promoting classroom discussions.

THE NEWSPAPER AND INNER-CITY TEACHING

One of the rewarding stories of the use of the newspaper in teaching has been its success among students in schools classified as "inner city." Several studies and programs have shown excellent results. One of the more promising findings concluded: "Positive changes in student attitudes toward community, school, and school subjects occurred during a four-week period in which newspapers were introduced in classrooms." (44) The systematically organized study, which involved 148 students in six classes in Houston, advises teachers in these environments to carefully consider adding this strategy to their teaching repertoire.

Some guidance for classroom procedures follows (16, 17):

Newspapers in general—Pupils should be taught to locate the who, what, when, why, and how of the news story.

Skimming—Skimming is a technique for finding information quickly. Newspaper exercises for developing this art include: getting information from a weather report; finding a name in the sports, obituary, or similar items; and looking for a job in the want ads.

Improving vocabulary—Newspapers use technical words in many fields. Pupils may list any such words they find and look up their meanings. Written and oral reports permit students to internalize and master the usage of these words. One educator prudently suggests, "Because disadvantaged-area pupils may find it difficult to speak to a group, the report is often written first."

Increasing reading speed—The newspaper format makes phrase-reading easier to grasp. Using phrasing from the newspaper and asking pupils to add a beginning or ending can be a valuable learning experience.

Writing—some specific ideas for writing exercises include:
1. Use a grocery ad to write a meal menu.
2. Write a letter in answer to an advertisement for a job.
3. Pretend you have have something to sell and write an advertisement for it.
4. Cut out a picture or cartoon and create a story about it.

Using graphic features—Normally maps appear in the newspaper which relate to an area in the news. These may be used to create a better understanding of place, location, and direction. Additionally, photographs, charts, and graphs may be studied to show how they aid in the clarification of news articles.

Mathematics—Some specific suggestions for student learning experiences include:
1. You have ten dollars. Buy an article of clothing you need. The sales tax is ____% and the cost of the item is _____. How much change will you receive?
2. Your family is shopping for a used car. What is the best price for the model you want? How much will you save by buying a good used car instead of a new one?

Guidance—Newspapers offer guidance in many areas—books, movies, theater, family living, etc. Such questions as the following are useful to ask the class with regard to the above: How well do the critics represent the feelings of the public? What factors determine their thinking on subjects?

Other educators have observed that "group work is very important when working with the newspaper. . . . Students are no longer just seeing facts and forgetting them—they are reading and becoming involved." (38)

One of the positive spin-off effects noted by inner-city educators has been parents' involvement in reading the newspaper. This common interest increased communication between parents and students and has improved school/community relationships. One project during National Fire Prevention Week resulted in students studying their homes for potential fire dangers and eliminating the hazards with their parents.

Unfortunately, some inner-city youth have never been enhanced by textbooks. Newspapers offer them an opportunity to successfully read and act on the events of the day. Attracting these students to reading the newspaper is particularly important in view of continuing research, which shows that those who do not read the newspaper are "related to the relatively lower levels of education and income." Many young adults fall in this category. (31) One group of educators noted: "Many of our poorer students, who had refused to read anything, turned into avid readers." (38)

READING

The newspaper's greatest appeal for many educators lies in its ability to improve reading skills. Researchers have clearly indicated that skillful and reflective use of the newspaper can stimulate a desire to read. One study of a nine-week program that experimented with the newspaper as a learning device reported significant gains in word recognition and in comprehension. (39) Another study with sixth graders using the newspaper on a daily basis concluded "that students exposed to the daily newspaper in the classroom out-performed those who pursued course work in the usual manner." (50) One factor that precipitated the study was the revelation that a very small percent of the average and below-average students at the school had a newspaper in their home, but almost all of the families of the above-average students regularly received a newspaper. This situation has been corroborated by another study, which found that 65 percent of the most intellectually capable eighth graders "read a newspaper every day," while only 30 percent of those less capable do. Among twelfth graders, 70 percent of the high achievers and 55 percent of the low achievers read the newspaper. (43)

In this regard, two studies are particularly significant. The first asked: Can a student become a better reader even if his family does not receive a daily newspaper at home? This study revealed "that whether or not the student is inherently familiar with the newspaper is irrelevant . . . most students can learn to read—and read to learn—better with a newspaper than with some other materials." (47)

The second study inquired: Will instruction in using the newspaper stimulate the students to read it outside of school? In responding to this question, juniors, seniors and graduates found "a significantly higher rate of daily newspaper reading" among those receiving instruction than those who were not. (36)

Teachers may use the following sample activity as a model or modify it (1, 4):

Activity
During the first class period, let the students handle the newspaper. On the second class day, ask the students to read or skim only those topics that interest them and then list the topics.

Questions to ask
1. What first attracts you to something in the newspaper? Habit? Headlines? Photographs?
2. Do you feel familiar enough with the paper to know which sections you prefer?
3. Are there other items in the newspaper that might interest you if you have more time?
4. Do you look at advertising? Why do you read an ad?

The newspaper headline, concentrating on the main idea of an article, may serve as an excellent focal point for a lesson with slower students. (1, 33)

Activity I
1. Create a newspaper of articles and photographs, but without headlines. Make multiple choices for distribution to the class.
2. Have the students write headlines for the articles.
3. Through the blackboard or transparency, share the students' headlines and use them as topics for discussion.

Activity II

Put a number of headline titles in an envelope and ask the students to match the appropriate one with an enclosed article. A number of envelopes may be made for use when students complete regular assignments. This activity may be modified for group activity by assigning each group one envelope and the task of choosing the correct headline. Whether individual or group, these activities should have a follow-up.

Other authors have listed the following activities to help students build reading skills (6, 11):

1. Read an article and note the five *W*s (who, what, where, when, why). Write a summary paragraph using this perspective.
2. Construct a time line or flow chart after a narrative article or a how-to article.
3. Follow a sports team by recording its program.
4. Use advertising supplements and classified ads to shop for clothes, gifts, cards, motorcycles, etc.
5. Follow the directions for a recipe.

Obviously, motivation is a critical component in working with the reluctant reader. Almost any section of the newspaper offers opportunities for classroom activities. One successful strategy involves career orientation. Career education has become a timely topic in many schools. Teachers should integrate this subject into courses whenever possible. The teacher may instruct the students to look at the help wanted section, observe the alphabetical order of each category, and learn what some of the abbreviations stand for—f/t, gd. oppty., exp. nec., sal., etc. The students should have many questions about the jobs listed. The teacher may also call attention to an advertisement and ask what jobs were necessary to produce the product advertised. (27) Ideally, the students' questions will stimulate further reading. Students also may be directed to consult the VGM Career Horizons series (National Textbook Company), which has become a staple in most school guidance counseling offices and libraries.

Given the importance of career education, it would seem that timing would not generally be a factor in planning for instruction. However, one teacher reported that timing was strategic in the area of career education: "To engage students in reading and remembering specific facts, have them use the 'help wanted' section of the paper prior to summer vacation." (11)

Several educators with extensive experience in using the newspaper to encourage reading have consistently emphasized the cost factor. Working in remedial reading, one teacher reported: "It was amazing to see how helpful an inexpensive item like the newspaper was for those tied up, poor readers."(22) Another stated: "The low cost of the newspaper is phenomenal." (7)

Research lends strong support for using the newspaper in reading programs. (35) One study described phenomenal results: "Seventh grade students involved in the program showed an average gain of 2.37 months for each month of instruction, or six times greater than the state average of .4 month gained per month of instruction for 7th grade Title Reading Programs, 1970–71." (42) Thus, the newspaper deserves the serious consideration of educators who are concerned with improving the skills of students.

ELEMENTARY EDUCATION

Although the simple basics of the newspaper form the basis for instructing students in the lower grades, an assessment of their knowledge will be very useful in determining how the newspaper should be used in the classroom. A questionnaire or a series of oral questions, which can be modified according to grade level, will reveal the extent of the students' knowledge. Such questions as the following should be helpful (40):

1. What newspapers are read by your parents? By yourself?
2. What sections do you read regularly? Occasionally?
3. Can you name any local papers?
4. Who is your favorite columnist?
5. What special terms are associated with newspapers?

Newspaper centers, like learning centers, may be established as part of a teacher's instructional strategy. The following activities may be used in a newspaper center. (15) Students may choose from various learning experiences grouped according to category.

How much will it cost?
The teacher places short shopping lists, including the amount to be spent, in an envelope pasted inside a folder. Students then select ads and recipes from the food section of the newspaper to perform one of the following activities:

14

1. Choose a shopping list from the envelope. Using the newspaper, cut out the items and prices of the things on the list. Glue the pictures into your scrapbook.
2. Add up the total of the items purchased and record the amount of money spent and the change received.
3. Cut out recipes from the food section. Paste them on cards and put them in the cooking center. Choose one recipe and make up a grocery list for it. Find these ingredients in the food ads. Add up their total cost.
4. Using the food ad, make up menus for a family of four for two days. Be sure to include the four basic food groups. How much will the meals cost?
5. Cut out all of the coupons in one paper. How much money would be saved if all of the coupons were used?

Using the index

The teacher pastes two or more newspaper indices inside a folder. Using an index to locate different information, students will learn that much time is saved. For example, the teacher may ask: On what pages will you find something about a famous person, a religious message, a word game, where a funeral is being held, the score of yesterday's basketball game, horoscopes, something funny, the stock prices, the editor's opinion, TV programs, the day of the week, and medical advice?

Aloha!

The teacher cuts out travel ads for resort areas and glues them on cards or construction paper. These are then numbered and placed in a folder with directions. Using these advertisements, the students are asked to answer the following questions: Which advertisement offers the best rates to Hawaii plus Las Vegas? Which one advertises the cheapest trip to Hawaii? Which ad mentions flying on a 747? Which one offers accommodations at Ala Moana Hotel? The students are then instructed to create their own ads for a Hawaiian tour, which will include writing a description of the tour, creating a company name, and listing travel rates.

The following suggestions may also be used for the basis of classroom activities or homework (40):

1. Find new words. Interpret their meaning from their context.
2. Summarize the science news for a week. What topic seems to be receiving the most coverage?
3. Collect news with geographic aspects.
4. Read and select new articles for cause and effect, main ideas, and implications.

Some elementary school educators have combined student interest in television with newspaper articles. This powerful combination strongly relates to student experience. Moreover, it may raise the level of the students' viewing skills by encouraging them to become more discriminating in their choice of programs.

One activity might involve the use of a bulletin board, where a group of students would daily clip from the newspaper items relating to television. In classifying these items, students would build inquiry decision-making skills. Such categories as TV stars, children's shows, the future of television, and parents' fears might be chosen by the students. (32)

Scripts of television shows have become increasingly popular. For example, in recent years newspapers have run the scripts of "Roots" and "The Ron La Flore Story" (professional baseball player). Some television companies will provide scripts of shows. Through a teacher's careful choice of the appropriate shows and segments of these shows, students can read in the newspaper a review of the show, read the script, view the program, and compare their analyses with that of the critic.

Comparing how a news story is covered on television and in the newspaper will frequently result in a discussion of the in-depth coverage possible in a newspaper, as opposed to the visual presentation television offers. Students will realize the special value of each medium and its role in our society. (32)

With younger children, newspaper photographs, illustrations, cartoons, and comics present many opportunities for various creative activities. Examples of their use follow (10):

1. They can be used for coloring.
2. They can be pasted on colored paper and used as flash cards to tell a story.
3. Pasteups can be perforated and strung together to make a comic or picture show.
4. Many newspapers contain puzzles, articles, and activities specifically designed for the young, for example, the minipage.

In the area of arithmetic, the newspaper offers young students countless opportunities. A sense for numbers may be developed by having students "count pages, columns on a page, articles on a page and headlines on a page." The large numbers used in advertisements are well suited for use by younger children. They can also cut out numbers from the newspaper to match numbers on a sheet provided by the teacher. (10)

Many other worthwhile activities will present themselves as teachers of primary grades introduce their pupils to the newspaper. The following list shows the response elementary teachers gave to a questionnaire asking: "In what ways have you used the newspaper with your students?'' (47) The topics appear according to those most often listed.

1. Arithmetic
2. Reading
3. Grammar and phonetics
· 4. Current events
5. Vocabulary
6. Studying the weather
7. Learning to give oral and written reports on topics in the newspaper
8. Studying social studies
9. Artistic use (coloring, pasting, collages, etc.)
10. Learning how a newspaper is put together
11. Homeroom
12. Stimulating sports interest
13. Learning how to plan a budget
14. Making personality reports
15. Graphing weather changes
16. Learning to read political cartoons
17. Making a news bulletin board
18. Using the supplements to match words with pictures
19. Using the advertising sections for large print in reading exercises
20. Studying where foods come from
21. Writing letters to the editor
22. Talking about advertising
23. Learning map skills
24. Creative writing from want ads
25. Reading the comics for a fun break
26. Language arts
27. Character studies
28. Shopping for groceries with a limited budget

SUBJECT AREAS

Social Studies

As an instructional tool, the newspaper is more easily incorporated into many social studies courses than into other subjects in the school curriculum. Some of the present trends in the social studies almost dictate using this medium in such programs. For example, many schools presently emphasize citizenship education; the newspaper becomes a natural tool in this regard. Unfortunately, some school students need considerable instruction in this area. Following a major study of thirteen thousand students in widely diverse areas of the country, the chief researcher remarked: "How safe is the country in the hands of people who—roughly speaking—understand only 50–60 percent of what they read in newspapers? Some effort to improve this showing is clearly needed." (12)

Current events has long been a focus of one aspect of citizenship education in the social studies. There exists some indication that it is not enough for teachers to simply present the newspaper to students. (9) Teachers must structure well-organized activities related to using the newspaper. Two teachers believe that the study of current events should be more than an unstructured "sharing period during which students contribute a motley assortment of news items while the teacher checks attendance." Rather, they suggest: "One method for organizing this type of reporting is through class committees. . . . Each committee may be given a specific geographic area on which to report—for example, local, regional, national or international news." (43)

Another suggestion directs the students to develop a "clipping thesis." The rationale for this exercise is that studying a situation over time is very effective in understanding contemporary affairs. The student first chooses an issue or problem. Over a designated period of time, the student clips and collects newspaper articles and photographs that appear on the subject. Then depending on the student's grade level and ability, the teacher may adopt the following activities (28):

Basic—The student pastes the clippings onto pages and writes a few descriptive sentences below each clipping. The pages are then attached to form a notebook, and a cover is made.

Intermediate—The student writes an introduction to the topic. A few carefully chosen articles, along with a commentary on each page, form the body of the book. Each of the articles should be from a different component of the topic. For example, in the area of the energy crisis, subtopics might be new sources, conservation, diplomacy, etc.

Advanced—The student writes an essay on the topic using the clippings as sources of information.

Research shows that well-organized and systematic teaching can make a tremendous difference. A very recent study indicated: "Students continuously exposed to the VEC program [see Resources section] scored much higher on the current affairs test than students . . . who had not yet been exposed to the VEC program." (3)

In the area of history, newspaper headlines are an excellent vehicle for introducing a new unit. (23) On a Thursday, the teacher may post the

18

headlines of several newspapers on the bulletin board before starting the new topic the following Monday. Many major newspapers periodically publish famous front pages for general promotional purposes or to stimulate the use of their newspaper in the schools. Teachers may wish to acquire previously published copies of these editions and should remain alert to obtain issues published on historic occasions.

The above activity may be individualized by having students obtain, through a mail-order house, the front page of the newspaper published on the day they were born. Students with access to library facilities may be able to obtain through microfilm several pages from such newspapers. These exercises offer an excellent opportunity for many learning experiences. (14)

The editorial cartoon has long enjoyed acceptance among teachers and students in the humanities. This type of art basically consists of an interpretative picture that makes use of symbolism and most often bold and humorous exaggeration to present a message or point of view concerning people, events, or situations. The editorial cartoon conveys its message quickly. (20) Recent years have seen a dramatic expansion of its use on standardized tests and in classrooms. Unfortunately, many people experience difficulty in understanding editorial cartoons. One study found that "newspaper editorial cartoonists are communicating with only a small percentage of the readers." The study further reported that "messages received by the people ran the gamut of meanings, and interpretations often differed markedly from the meanings intended by the cartoonist." (5)

For many reasons, the editorial cartoon should be included in the content and methodology used in social studies classes. It may be used (1) to help students better understand a historical event or contemporary problem or (2) as an aid in comprehending the medium itself. Using editorial cartoons in the classroom has several distinct values. Following projection of a cartoon the teacher may ask: What is the message of the cartoonist? Do you agree? Two cartoons with opposing viewpoints may be shown and the students may be asked: Which one do you agree with? Why? Some other activities may involve distributing a cartoon without a title and asking the students to create a title; directing the students to choose a topic and then draw a cartoon (stick figures acceptable) of their own; and maintaining a bulletin board collection of cartoons. (21, 25)

Frequently, timing is a major factor in successfully incorporating use of the newspaper into the social studies classroom. During political campaigns, the newspaper serves as an excellent guide to elections. Reading the newspaper regularly can help the student to develop skills and acquire knowledge in many of the new areas of emphasis in history and the social sciences.

English and Communication Arts

As with the social studies, the newspaper is a natural tool in teaching English and the communication arts. Vocabulary building, writing activities, literature, theater, and reading are all intimately connected with the newspaper.

One educator, confronted with "150 high school juniors, none of whom could read a seventh grade literature book," found that the newspaper is much more than a pleasant adjunct to the English curriculum. It can *be* the English curriculum. "Furthermore, it pleased the students because the newspaper looks nothing like a textbook and carried no remedial reading stigma." (18) In a similar vein, another English teacher found: "Lethargy can be dispelled to a great extent if the teacher exploits the local newspaper." (37)

Grammar skills may be taught through the application of the following group activity. Select newspaper articles and delete the verbs in several sentences. Divide the students into groups according to some prearranged scheme (i.e., according to intellectual ability, popularity among peers, etc.). Give each group some of the articles with the missing verbs and ask them to fill in the blanks. When they finish, give them the original article to compare with their suggestions. Share some of the groups' choices with the class. (1)

Building writing skills through assigning students to compose letters to the editor of a newspaper has long been a successful instructional method. Often these letters are the response to reactions to international, national, and local problems. While designed as an exercise, writing these letters will frequently result in publication if submitted to the local newspaper. (24)

The newspaper unit serves as one of the important components of the English curriculum. This unit involves studying the newspaper itself, as opposed to using it as a vehicle to obtain knowledge or skills in another area. The Glossary of Newspaper-Related Terms in this publication will be helpful in this regard. The following activities may serve as examples of methods that may be used with this unit.

The scavenger hunt provides students the opportunity to obtain a knowledge of and locate the various sections of the newspaper. The teacher may make a list of the sections of a newspaper, duplicate and distribute it among the students, and instruct the students to use the newspaper, placing the appropriate page numbers next to each section. A follow-up activity might involve listing the titles of articles and directing the students to locate and record the page numbers where the articles are found. Having already familiarized themselves with the various sections within the newspaper, the students should first consult the appropriate sections while searching for the articles. These activities should be modified according to the students' grade level and ability. (49)

Comparing newspapers can be a very stimulating classroom activity that will enable students to obtain an in-depth knowledge of the newspaper in general. The newspapers to be used may be local or national. The library reference shelf lists several works that provide addresses. Once the newspapers are collected, groups of students may examine the various sections—business, sports, obituaries, etc.—then report on their section to the class. (13) Another strategy involves giving each student the assignment of obtaining, displaying in class, and reporting on a newspaper. The student would provide information on such areas as title, location, number of pages, frequency of publication, cost, circulation, format, pages devoted to each department, photographs, editorial bias, treatment of local news vis-à-vis national news, and evaluation of the paper. (30)

Another area of interest to students that offers a fertile ground for instruction is advertising. A quick search through the newspaper reveals examples of various types of appeals to the public—testimonials, glittering generalities, band wagon, plain folks, and others. From the newspaper, clip an example of each, duplicate the examples, and share them with the class. Teachers can then instruct their students to write ads; propose such related topics of discussion as how a consumer may be informed; and deliver short lectures, including information on the role of advertising in newspapers—i.e., on the average, newspapers receive 75 percent of their income from advertising sales. (10, 41)

Field trips to newspapers, constructing a classroom newspaper, guest lectures, and holding a simulated press conference are but a few of the myriad activities available for teaching about the newspaper. In English and communication arts, the newspaper exists as a double-barreled tool to promote knowledge and skills among interested young people.

Other Areas

While the newspaper more clearly relates to the social sciences, English, and communication arts, it also may be applied to other areas. The newspaper may also further motivate students in these fields. The newspaper regularly contains a host of current events in the field of science. Scientific achievements receive expanded coverage. Often, a newspaper will provide a chronicle of the developments that resulted in a scientific discovery. Such items as these may be clipped by students and used for reports. For example, the expanding energy crisis dictates close coverage by the media. Similarly, information on the environment, space travel, the oceans, and similar subjects is provided regularly in the newspaper.

Graphs, charts, and illustrations are teaching materials frequently used in arithmetic courses. Advertisements, the stock market, and government budgets offer information for building mathematical skills. The following may serve as sample lessons (26):

1. Ask the students to collect travel ads. Then, using a library reference, ask them to obtain the mileage between locations and compute the cost per mile for each ad.
2. Direct the students to use the advertising page to calculate the cost of an item of two different sizes to obtain a per-ounce price.

Some art-related current events appear in the paper. However, the art teacher should make a special effort to obtain newspaper clippings for student use. Drawing editorial cartoons forms the basis for an interdisciplinary link between art and social studies if a social problem is chosen as the object. Young students will enjoy constructing collages, while older students may write newspaper-style critiques of local exhibits. An exercise in advertising design and layout may take the following form: "Do any advertisement for a space 3 x 7 to sell this product." (27) Other students may wish to create a comic strip. With younger children, lessons in such concepts and skills as color recognition, cutting and pasting, using a ruler, and weaving can easily be accomplished through using a newspaper. (34)

Home economics teachers will find their students' curiosities aroused by designing such activities as comparison of prices in ads. Recipes, sources of sales, personal advice, consumer protection, recent developments in the field, and family recreation opportunities may all be found in the newspaper. One lesson may involve students drawing a floor plan for a house. The Sunday real estate section offers various ideas for this activity. Obtaining from the Government Printing Office a list of new publications will advance a student's knowledge of the most recent information available. Other lessons may develop accordingly.

The public's increasing interest in health, nutrition, and physical fitness has not been ignored in the newspaper. In addition to columns offering medical and health advice, contemporary developments appear not only in the sports section but throughout the newspaper. The following format may be incorporated into model lessons (26):

1. Assign a health-related topic (vitamins, cigarette smoking, chemical hazards, cancer developments) to each student to clip articles on a post on one of the classroom bulletin boards reserved for them.
2. Assign a group of students to make a chart on deaths in the local community. Through using the obituary section, gender, age, and cause of death may be plotted if all of the information is provided.

With some imagination and effort, the newspaper will successfully serve many disciplines. One publisher even prints excerpts and exercises from foreign-language newspapers for use in teaching (see Resources section of this publication).

CONCLUSION

On a recent Tuesday morning, Bill Ray Tolland walked into his classroom with a stack of *USA Todays* under his arm. Tolland, a seventh grade teacher at the Columbia Terrace School, was immediately approached by Ricky Manley, one of his students. "Can I look at the paper for a couple of minutes?" the boy asked. When Ricky quickly opened it to the day's weather map, Tolland asked, "What are you looking for?" "We have a baseball game after school today and I wanted to see if it was going to rain." Tolland mused to himself, "A couple of weeks ago Ricky was reluctant to took at any reading material and never would have thought to look for information in the paper. The newspaper unit has been both a cognitive and an affective success."

Tolland's experience is not isolated; researchers tell us that students enjoy using the newspaper in the classroom and profit from it. A number of examinations (B, D, N, O, Q)* have shown many student gains from this activity. Students grow in their knowledge of current events, they improve their reading comprehension skills, they develop the newspaper reading habit, and they build a wide variety of basic skills. Furthermore, the success of a well-organized and effectively taught newspaper program is not limited to the elementary and secondary level; a number of studies (F, K) have shown success with college students, and the potential for use with adults may be the wave of the future (M).

The growing desire to deal with the problem of adult illiteracy makes the newspaper a natural. An adult activity, reading the newspaper does not carry the stigma of some materials used to teach reading. Undoubtedly, the major new focus of NIE will become adult literacy programs—offered by schools, churches and synagogues, prisons, iibraries, and similar organizations.

In the years ahead as educators' success is closely monitored by the public, teachers at all levels working with all ability groups will find success in using the newspaper in the classroom.

---

*See Additional References for the Second Edition on page 32.

RESOURCES

Aguilar, Felipa. *Bilingual Expression: A Doorway to Understanding through the* Houston Post. *The Houston Post,* 4747 Southwest Freeway, Houston, Texas 77001. Designed to aid students with various levels of competence in English as a second language, this teacher's guide includes several activities of varying levels.

American Newspaper Publishers Association Foundation. P.O. Box 17407, Dulles International Airport, Washington, D.C. 20041. This source of information on using the newspaper in teaching will also be helpful in identifying a newspaper educator in your region.

Ayers Directory of Publications. Ayers Press, 210 Washington Square, Philadelphia, Pennsylvania 19106. A library reference listing the nation's newspapers' addresses, this directory may be used to obtain papers for comparison.

Brownstein, Alexandra. *Career Education Program* (1974). College and School Services, *New York Times,* 229 West 43d Street, New York, New York 10036. Contains many activities demonstrating how the newspaper serves as a virtual supermarket for career education projects. The U.S. Office of Education Guidelines provide the structure for the materials.

Cheyney, Arnold. *Teaching Reading Skills through the Newspaper* (1972). International Reading Association, P.O. Box 8139, Newark, Delaware 19711. Deals with the field of reading and how the newspaper can aid readers of all abilities.

Cooperative Tests and Services, Educational Testing Service, Princeton, New Jersey 08540. The source of the ANPA Foundation's newspaper test. The examination measures student's knowledge of the newspaper and how to read it.

Edens, Glynnane, and Sandifer, Ann. *Newspaper: A Natural Bridge to English as a Second Language. El Paso Times* and *El Paso Herald-Post,* P.O. Box Drawer 20, El Paso, Texas 79999. Provides a variety of graduated practical materials.

Gentry, Carolyn. *Photo-Journalism* (1976). *Florida Times-Union,* 1 Riverside Avenue, Jacksonville, Florida 32217. This booklet contains a history of the subject as well as suggested lessons and ideas on interpreting photographs.

Heitzmann, Wm. Ray. *50 Political Cartoons for Teaching American History* (1975). J. Weston Walch, P.O. Box 658, Portland, Maine 04104. An inexpensive series of carefully selected editorial cartoons, with each series containing background information and suggested teaching ideas.

Jacobs, Jo Ann. *Elementary Activities for Using the Newspaper* (1978). *Detroit Free Press,* 321 Fayette Boulevard, Detroit, Michigan 48231. A collection of 225 cards in various subject areas for use by students independently or with teacher involvement.

Learning Activities for Primary Grades (1978). *Independent Press-Telegram,* P.O. Box 230, Long Beach, California 90844. Offers hints for using the paper with young students in many fields.

Newspaper. National Textbook Company, 8259 Niles Center Road, Skokie, Illinois 60076. A series of books on spirit masters, in French, Italian, and Spanish, containing excerpts from newspapers that form lessons in foreign language development and cultural knowledge.

Newspaper in the Classroom (1970). *New York Daily News,* 220 East 42d Street, New York, New York 10017. A comprehensive booklet that relates to the tabloid format.

Newspaper Unit: Elementary Level (1976). *San Jose Mercury and News,* 750 Ridder Park Drive, San Jose, California 95190. Provides lesson plans and information for a two-week unit for younger students.

Lohmann, Idella. *Open Windows to the World through the Living Textbook* (1975). *Daily Oklahoman and Times,* P.O. Box 25125, Oklahoma City, Oklahoma 73125. Presents several activities for students of many ages and abilities.

Partlow, Hugh. *Learning from Newspapers* (1976). Canadian Daily Newspaper Publishers Association, Suite 214, 321 Bloor Street, East, Toronto, Ontario M4W 1E7. A general reference to teaching about newspapers.

_____. *Learning from Newspapers: Reading* (1976). This book focuses on the development of reading competence through continued daily use of the newspaper.

Piercey, Dorothy, ed. Newspaper in Education (1976). *Arizona Republic* and *Phoenix Gazette,* P.O. Box 1950, Phoenix, Arizona 85110. A series of booklets on a range of topics beneficial to elementary and secondary teaching, such as The Newspaper and Business Law.

Teacher's Guide: High School Social Studies (1973). Evansville Printing Corporation, 201 N.W. Second Street, Evansville, Indiana 47702. A small book containing a diverse range of topics, activities, and references.

Using the Daily Newspaper To. . . . The Hawaii Newspaper Agency, P.O. Box 3350, Honolulu, Hawaii 96801. A series of twenty booklets covering various grade levels and subjects areas, such as teaching adults.

Verner, Zenobia. *Newsbook of Reading Comprehension Activities* (1978). Clayton Publishing Co., 4384 Wheeler, Houston, Texas 77004. A selection of activities for the reader already possessing some basic skill but needing additional learning experiences (secondary, adult).

Visual Education Consultants. P.O. Box 52, Madison, Wisconsin 53701. This organization offers a filmstrip of the previous week's news, an accompanying teacher's guide for thirty-five weeks, a filmstrip and guide on an in-depth topic for ten months, and a kit with suggested activities for using the newspaper. These materials are paid for by the cooperating newspaper in the school's locality, and the school receives a discount on the papers. Back issues of materials are available.

GLOSSARY OF
NEWSPAPER-RELATED TERMS

ad–advertisement

advance–story concerning a forthcoming newsworthy event

AP (Associated Press)–a news-gathering service that provides worldwide news

beat—assignment a reporter regularly covers, for example, sports, religion, or police news

blow up—expand a story; to play up or feature an event

byline—name of the writer of the story that appears under the title

columnist—writer who uses the same location in the paper on a regular basis

copy—written material

dateline—indication at the beginning of the story of its origin and location

editorial—article that expresses the opinion of the editors and usually the publisher (owner) of the paper

editorial cartoon (political cartoon)—cartoon that expresses an opinion on a situation or issue

extra—additional or special edition published because a particularly outstanding event merits it

filler—short news item that serves to fill out the space on a page

First amendment—constitutional amendment guaranteeing, among other freedoms, freedom of the press

follow-up—story giving additional developments of an event covered in a previous edition

Fourth Estate—of European origin, this term is used for the media, particularly newspaper people

hard news—news reported without much background or interpretation

libel—written statement that injures a person's reputation (the author of the statement may be sued, and the injured person may be awarded a financial settlement)

library—newspaper's collection of clippings on various topics to be used for research on future articles

national advertising—ads on products that are sold throughout the nation

obituary (obit)—biography of a recently deceased person (the size usually varies with the person's prominence)

op ed—page opposite the editorial page on which articles by national columnists and local personalities are printed, along with letters to the editor

press agent—public relations person who acts on behalf of an organization to provide publicity to the news media

press conference—meeting called to present information to the media, usually in the form of a press release, presentation, statement, and questions

press release—written statement prepared for the media, normally delivered by mail

proofreader—person who reads galley proofs (samples of how the newspaper will look) and corrects errors

review—evaluation of a book, play, movie, or other cultural event

tabloid—newspaper whose page size is smaller than usual (such as the *Chicago Sun-Times, National Enquirer,* and the *New York Daily News*

UP (United Press International)—news-gathering service that provides worldwide news

yellow journalism—term applied to stories or newspapers that feature sensationalism to promote sales

SELECTED REFERENCES

1. American Newspaper Publishers Association Foundation. *The Newspaper as an Effective Teaching Tool.* Washington, D.C.: American Newspapers Publishers Association Foundation, 1975.
2. Berryman, Charles. *Improving Reading Skills.* Atlanta: The Atlanta Journal-Constitution, 1973.
3. Belden, Joseph, et al. *"The Bulletin* VEC School Program: A Test of Effectiveness." Dallas: Belden Associates, 1979.
4. Butters, Jane, et al. *Innovate.* Chicago: Chicago Tribune Company, 1974.
5. Carl, Leroy. "Editorial Cartoons Fail to Reach Readers." *Journalism Quarterly* 45:533-535; 1968; and Brinkman, Del. "Do Editorial Cartoons and Editorials Change Opinion." *Journalism Quarterly* 45: 723-734; 1968.
6. Charry, Myrna, Bateman, Kitty, and Feiberger. *The New York Times Reading Experience.* New York: New York Times Company, 1978.
7. Cheyney, Arnold. *Teaching Reading Skills through the Newspaper.* Newark, Del.: International Reading Association, 1971.
8. Cook, Sandra. *Using Reading Skill with the Newspaper to Develop Ideational Fluency.* Ph.D. dissertation. Durham, N.C.: Duke University, 1977.
9. Daniel, Elbert. *An Evaluation of the Iowa "Newspapers in the Classrooms of a Free Society" Workshops and an Assessment of the Impact of Newspaper Instruction.* Ph.D. dissertation. Ames: University of Iowa, 1972.
10. Decker, Howard. "Five Dozen Ideas for Teaching the Newspaper Unit." *English Journal* 56:268-272; and Haefner, John. "The Daily Newspaper in the School Curriculum." Washington, D.C.: American Newspaper Publishers Association Foundation, March, 1967.
11. Degler, Lois. "Using the Newspaper to Develop Reading Comprehension Skills." *Journal of Reading* 21:339-342; January 1978.
12. Diederich, Paul. "Effects of the 'Newspaper in the Classroom' Program on Understanding Newspapers." Press release. Princeton, N.J.: Educational Testing Service, 1971.
13. Downing, Edna. *Units on the Study of the Newspaper.* Washington, D.C.: American Newspaper Publishers Association Foundation, 1961.
14. Epstein, Ira. "What Happened on the Day You Were Born?" *Journal of Reading* 20:400-402; February 1977.
15. Fairleigh, Roberts. "Extra! Extra! The Newspaper Center." *Teacher* 95:50-55; February 1977.
16. Fasan, Walter, and Isbitz, Helen. "Reading Activities Using Newspapers." *Instructor* 76:24-25, 49; January 1967.
17. Fidell, Jeannette, and Horn, Valerie. *The New York Times for Reluctant Readers.* New York: New York Times Co., n.d.
18. Flynn, Peggy. "What's Black and White and Spread All Over? The Newspaper." *Journal of Reading* 21:725-728; May 1978.
19. Haffey, Kay. "It's Black and White and Read All Over." *Pennsylvania School Journal* 127:22-26; October 1978.

20. Heitzmann, Wm. Ray. "The Political Cartoon and the Social Science Teacher." *Social Studies* 65:10-11; February 1974.

21. _____."The Political Cartoon as a Teaching Device." *Teaching Political Science* 6:166-184; January 1979.

22. Johnson, Laura. "The Newspaper: A New Textbook Every Day, Part I, II." *Journal of Reading* 11:107-112, 164; November 1968 and 11:203-206, 240-245; December 1968.

23. _____. "The Newspaper as an Instructional Medium." *Teachers, Tangibles, Techniques: Comprehension of Content in Reading.* (Edited by Donnie Schulwitz.) Newark, Del.: International Reading Association, 1975.

24. Leeson, Jeanne. "Newspapers Sell Communication Skills." *Instructor* 80:105-106; January 1971.

25. Matlack, Harry. "Teaching Use of the Newspaper." *Clearing House* 35:92-95; October 1960.

26. *Newspaper as a Teaching Tool, The.* Madison, Wis.: Visual Educational Consultants, n.d.; Washington, D.C.: National Institute of Education Resource Unit, 1978.

27. *New York Times Career Education Program.* New York: New York Times Company, n.d.

28. *"New York Times* Clipping Thesis." New York: New York Times Company, n.d.

29. Norman, Betty, "Changes in Verbal Interaction as a Result of Newspaper's Instructional Use." Unpublished monograph. The University of Houston and American Newspaper Publishers Association Foundation. Westbury, Ian, and Bellack, Arno. *Research into Classroom Processes.* New York: Teachers College Press, 1971.

30. *Practical Suggestions for Using the Newspaper in Classrooms of Elementary, Junior and Senior High Schools.* St. Louis: St. Louis Globe-Democrat, n.d.

31. Penrose, Jeanne, et al. "The Newspaper Non-reader 10 Years Later: A Partial Replication of Wesley-Severin." *Journalism Quarterly* 51:631-638; 1974; and Schweitzer, John C. "Comparison of Young Subscribers and Non-subscribers to Newspapers." *Journalism Quarterly* 53:287-292; 1976.

32. Potter, Rosemary. "The Newspaper-TV Connection: A Way to Teach Skills." *Teacher* 95:36-38; December 1977.

33. *Reading, Writing, Language, Literature.* Chicago: Chicago Tribune Company, 1977.

34. Reschke, Luvella, and Reschke, Alfred. *The Newspaper in the Classroom.* Milwaukee: E. W. Hale, 1939.

35. Ross, Sandra. "The Effect of Using the Newspaper to Teach Reading to a Select Group of Sixth-Grade Students with Below Average Reading Ability." Unpublished monograph. Washington, D.C.: American Newspaper Publishers Association Foundation; and Rowe, Linda. "The Newspaper in the English Classroom: A Study of the Effects of Using the Daily Newspaper as a Tool for Teaching Selected Basic Reading Skills to Low-Level Ability High School Students." Unpublished monograph. Washington, D.C.: American Newspaper Publishers Association Foundation, October 1977.

36. Rowe, Linda. "The Results of an Informal Survey of the Newspaper Reading Habits of Selected NIE and Non-NIE Students." Unpublished monograph. Washington, D.C.: American Newspaper Publishers Association Foundation, 1977.
37. Salama, Nancy. "Use the Newspaper." *English Language Teaching Journal* 28:336-343; July 1974.
38. Soverly, Ron. "The Newspaper as a Tool for Teaching Kids to Read." *Phi Delta Kappa* 57:260-261; December 1975.
39. Stetson, Elton, et al. "The Effectiveness of Newspaper Use on Reading Achievement of Secondary Special Education Students." ED 149 536. Bethesda, Md.: ERIC, 1977.
40. Stewart, Miller. "Newspapers: Thinking Child's Textbook." *Instructor* 76:23-25; May 1967.
41. Stocks, Patricia. "Impression of the Penny Press." *Journal of Reading* 19:388-390; February 1975.
42. Title I Reading Project Ector County Grades 7-8, 1971-72. Odessa, Texas.
43. Tiedt, Sidney, and Tiedt, Iris. "Teaching Current Events." *Social Studies* 58:112-114; March 1967; and Schramm, Wilbur, Lyle, Jack, and Parker, Edwin B. "Patterns in Children's Reading of Newspapers." *Journalism Quarterly* 53:35-44; 1960.
44. Verner, Zenobia, and Murphy, Louis. "Does the Use of the Newspaper in the Classroom Affect Attitudes of Students?" *Clearing House* 50:350-351; April 1977.
45. Wardell, Patricia. *The Development and Evaluation of a Reading Program Designed to Improve Specific Skills through Reading a Newspaper.* Ph.D. dissertation. Boston University School of Education, 1973.
47. Using Newspapers in Reading Programs for Disadvantaged Students, 1969-1970-1971." Rochester, N.Y.: Gannett Rochester Newspapers, n.d.
49. Whisler, Nancy. "The Newspapers: Resource for Teaching Study Skills." *Reading Teacher* 25:652-656; April 1972.
50. Wilson, Al. "Sixth Grade Students Gain Four Months on Control Group." *Grassroots Editor* (1966 reprint).
51. Yamakawa, Alan. *Survival Teaching.* Chicago: Chicago Tribune Company, 1974; and Sanders, Norris. *Classroom Questions: What Kinds?* New York: Harper and Row, 1966.

ADDITIONAL REFERENCES FOR THE SECOND EDITION

A. Anderson, Thelma. *Assessing the Impact of Newspapers in Educational Programs: Changes in Students' Attitudes, Newspaper Reading and Political Awareness,* Newspaper Readership Project Research Report. New York: Newspaper Advertising Bureau, 1982.

B. Beals, Paul E. "The Newspaper in the Classroom: A Rationale for Its Use." *Reading World* 23:69-70; October 1983.

C. _____. "The Newspaper in the Classroom: Some Notes on Recent Research." *Reading World* 23:381-82; May 1984.

D. Callahan, Tim, and Felton, Randall. "The Newspaper in the Social Studies Classroom: An Issue-Oriented Curriculum." ED 221 879. ERIC 1980.

E. De Roche, Edward F. "Newspaper in Education: What We Know." *Newspaper Research Journal* 2:59-63; April 1981.

F. Detzner, Daniel F. "Developing the News Habit in the Introductory American Government Course." *Teaching Political Science* 9:177-84; Summer 1982.

G. Futhey, Carol, and Mazey, Mary E. "Classroom Strategies for Using the Newspaper." Paper presented at annual meeting of National Council for Geographic Education, San Diego, Calif., 1982.

H. Geyer, Ruth. "Teacher Research Study." *San Francisco Examiner.* Newspaper in Education Program, 1979.

I. Guthrie, John. "How We Understand the News." *Journal of Reading* 23:162-64; 1979.

J. Haefner, John H. "Partners in Education: The Newspaper as a Source in the Classroom." Washington, D.C.: American Newspaper Publishers Association Foundation, 1983.

K. Kelley, Allen C. "The Newspaper Can Be an Effective Tool." *Journal of Economic Education* 14:56-58; Fall 1983.

L. Kerr, Karen. "Read All About It: Developing Newspaper Skills." Iowa Area Education Agency 7, 1980. ED 230 204. ERIC 1980.

M. Lawson, V. K., et al. "Read All About It: Tutor Adults with the Daily Newspaper." Rochester, N.Y.: Gannett Foundation, 1984.

N. "The Newspaper as an Effective Teaching Tool: A Brief Introduction to the Newspaper in Education Concept." Washington, D.C.: American Newspaper Publishers Association Foundation, 1983.

O. "The Newspaper in Education: What It Does to Children's Civic Awareness and Attitudes Toward Newspapers." Newspaper Readership Project. Washington, D.C.: American Newspaper Publishers Association Foundation, 1982.

P. Oates Rita H. "Newspaper Quiz Is a Weekly Stimulus to Better Writing." *Journalism Educator* 38:24-26; Summer 1983.

Q. Seely, Patricia B. "Reading Comprehension Benefits from Use of Newspaper with Texts." *Phi Delta Kappan* 61:494; 1980.

R. Sokol, Kristin R. "Newspaper Index Poster." *Journal of Reading* 29:637; 1985.